LEGACIES
ARCHITECTURE

Richard Wood

Wayland

Legacies

Architecture
Clothes and Fashion
Language and Writing
Science and Technology
Sports and Entertainment
Politics and Government

Cover: The ancient Pyramids at Giza, Egypt (main) and the modern pyramid outside the Louvre in Paris, France (inset). The strength and simplicity of the pyramid shape still inspire us after 5,000 years.

Series editor: Polly Goodman
Book researcher: Katherine Thomson
Series designer: Liz Miller
Book designer: Malcolm Walker

First published in 1994 by
Wayland (Publishers) Limited
61 Western Road, Hove
East Sussex BN3 1JD, England

British Library Cataloguing in Publication Data
    Wood, Richard
    Architecture. – (Legacies Series)
    I. Title II. Bull, Peter III. Series
    720.9

ISBN 0 7502 1272 1

Typeset by Kudos Editorial and Design Services
Printed and bound in Italy by G.Canale C.S.p.A., Turin

Contents

Legacies are things that are handed down from an ancestor or predecessor. The modern world has inherited many different legacies from ancient civilizations. This book explores the architectural legacies of the ancient world.

Ancient Celts

c.750 BC – AD 100

Celtic round houses of wattle and daub and thatched roofs were built across much of Europe as Celtic tribes spread and settled in areas they conquered.

Monument Builders

c.2500 – 1000 BC

The massive stone circle of Stonehenge in southern England is a legacy left by the prehistoric monument builders. Monuments were built by people right across western Europe to honour their gods as they settled in communities.

Ancient Rome

c.507 BC – AD 476

The Romans developed the arch and the vault to build huge structures such as aqueducts and amphitheatres. The Colosseum amphitheatre (right) was home to the Roman Games, spectacles where gladiators and wild animals fought to the death.

ANCIENT CIVILIZATIONS

This is where the ancient civilizations described in this book were. The approximate dates of the peak of each civilization are given under each heading. You can find the exact areas at the beginning of each civilization's chapter.

Ancient Greece

c.800 – 331 BC

Overlooking the city of Athens, the Acropolis, meaning 'high city', was a sacred place with temples and shrines to the goddess Athene. Athens was a powerful city state and became the centre of Greek civilization and culture in the fifth century BC.

Ancient Middle East
Sumerians c.3500 – 2400 BC
Canaanites c.2500 – 1200 BC
Babylonians c.1900 – 539 BC
Phoenicians c.1200 – 146 BC
Hebrews c.1200 BC – onwards
The Marsh Arabs who live in present-day Iraq still build reed houses like those of their ancient ancestors. The ancient Middle East was home to many ancient civilizations, including the Sumerians, Canaanites and Babylonians, who built the first cities.

Ancient Asia
Mauryan dynasty, India c.322–185 BC
Ch'in dynasty, China c.221–206 BC
T'ang dynasty, China c.AD 618–906
Buddhist stupas, like these in Sri Lanka, were built in the eastern civilizations of ancient India and China, in sacred places connected with the Buddha's life. The stupa developed into the curved roofed pagoda, which became the distinctive architectural style of Asia.

Ancient Egypt
c.3100 – 30 BC
The ancient Egyptians built great pyramid tombs to bury their pharaohs in. This sphinx, with a lion's body, lies outside King Khafre's pyramid to act as guardian to his tomb.

chisel   set square

hammer   plumbline

These were some of the working tools of the Egyptian pyramid builders, 4,500 years ago. A modern builder's tool kit contains some remarkably similar items.

chapter one

ARCHITECTURE: MODERN AND ANCIENT

Architecture is all around us. It can be seen in the different types and styles of buildings we see every day. Architecture most affects us in the domestic buildings, or homes, where we, our friends and neighbours live. Homes may come in many shapes and sizes. Their design depends on things such as the wealth and size of the family, their lifestyle, the country's climate, and what building materials are available nearby. These things have always affected the design of homes, ever since the earliest prehistoric peoples began to settle in family and community groups. Building homes is one of the most basic practices we have inherited from our ancient ancestors.

Some buildings which are in the same area are much older than others. Many ancient structures are now buried underground, and we have to rely on archaeologists to uncover foundations, floors and walls of buildings buried beneath the earth. However some ancient architecture, even from prehistoric times, is still standing, either as ruins or as more complete structures. A few ancient buildings are still in use, 2,000 years or more after they were constructed.

◄ *The ancient city of Rome is modern Italy's capital. The forum was an important meeting place in ancient Rome. Its ruins still show its ancient architecture.*

But there is another sort of legacy, too. This consists of ancient ideas and designs, skills and methods. Some have come down to us through the ages by continuous use. Others were forgotten about, perhaps for centuries, and then rediscovered later on in history. The use of the plug and socket is an ancient building technique. It was how the Stone Age builders of Stonehenge, England, joined their massive stones together. The ancient Greeks used a similar method to join stone blocks into tall columns. The Celts, in Scotland and Ireland, cut wooden joints to connect the sections of their timber-framed houses. Today, builders often still rely on this basic technique for fixing sections of buildings together.

▼ *The great monuments of modern cities can be surprisingly similar to those of ancient times. Here, in Washington DC, USA, you can see an Egyptian-style obelisk, a Greek-style temple and a Roman-style dome.*

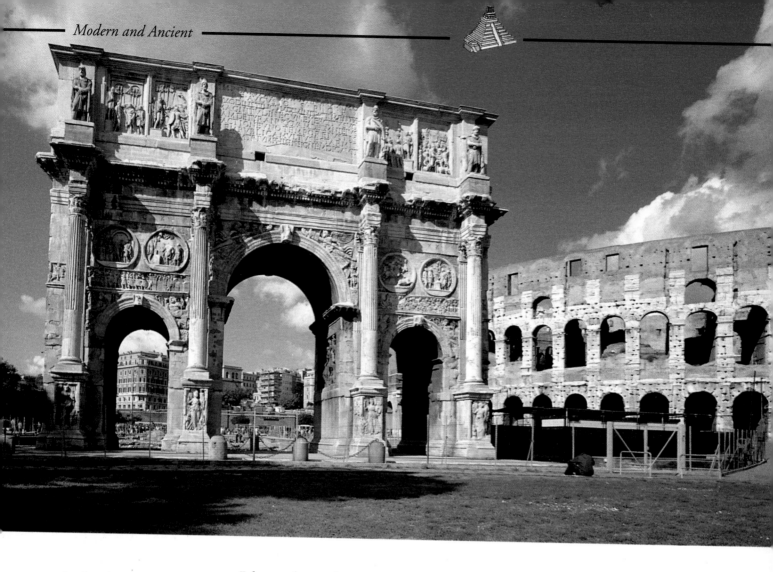

▲ *Ancient builders, like modern ones, sometimes re-used designs and materials from older buildings. The Roman Emperor Constantine took pieces from buildings all over Rome to construct this arch in AD 315.*

Ideas about beauty also take us back to ancient times. In the western world, rules about balance and proportion in design, which the Greeks first worked out almost 3,000 years ago, still influence the look of many buildings, from small houses to great public works. In Asia, traditional forms and techniques, like the curved roofs of pagodas, are often still used to decorate new buildings.

Our building materials, too, may have an ancient ancestry. Our choice of materials still depends largely on what can be found or made locally, whether it is stone, timber, brick or mud. Modern transport and new inventions have widened the choice for builders today, at least in richer countries. But despite this, many ancient techniques, like the thatching and tiling of roofs, are still widely used.

Other traditional skills, like timber framing, have been adapted for modern buildings. Bricks and concrete, two of the most widely used materials of all, are both ancient inventions which have been continuously used ever since.

The legacy of ancient architecture may be in your street or in your town. Many buildings, even new ones, can give clues about their ancestry. Look for rectangular windows, pillars and pediments (from Greece), arches, domes and curved roof tiles (from Rome), timbers which slot together (from Stone Age and Celtic times) and curvy shapes (from Asia). See how much we still rely on bricks (introduced in the ancient Middle East) and concrete (a Roman invention). You may be surprised at how great the legacy of ancient architecture is.

▶ A piece of ancient Egypt in the heart of a modern city. Cleopatra's Needle was taken to England in the nineteenth century and stands on the bank of the River Thames in London. The Needle began a fashion for modern monuments shaped like it, called an obelisk shape.

▼ *The architect Edwin Lutyens designed this First World War memorial at Thiepval, France, to remind people of a Roman triumphal arch.*

chapter two

MONUMENT BUILDERS

▲ *Every gravestone in the Arlington National Cemetery in Virginia, USA is a monument to the life of a human being.*

Monuments are objects set up to celebrate or remember things. We rarely have to travel far in the modern world to find monuments. Sometimes they are quite small, like gravestones or statues. They remind future generations of the life of one person. Sometimes they are bigger, like war memorials, designed to remind us of many people or important events. Great cities often have huge monuments which have become landmarks known all over the world, like the Eiffel Tower in Paris and the Statue of Liberty at the entrance to New York harbour. These monuments remind us of the pride people felt in their achievements and freedoms.

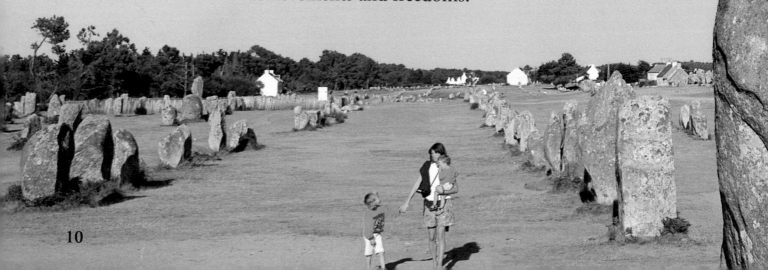

The urge to build monuments is something shared by most peoples worldwide since prehistoric times. The earliest monuments of all are among the best-known structures that have ever been built by human beings.

Prehistoric monuments are all over the world. In Europe alone there are about 50,000 separate monuments. The ideas and skills of building them seem to have arrived with the first farmers from the Middle East, after 6000 BC. As people relied less on hunting and gathering for food, they settled in communities. They learned how to build fixed homes to live in, and often built monuments too.

Some of these Stone Age monuments consist of passages and tombs cut into rock under earth mounds. The tombs at Hal Safliene on the Mediterranean island of Malta were made almost 5,000 years ago. They held the remains of 7,000 bodies, hidden underground.

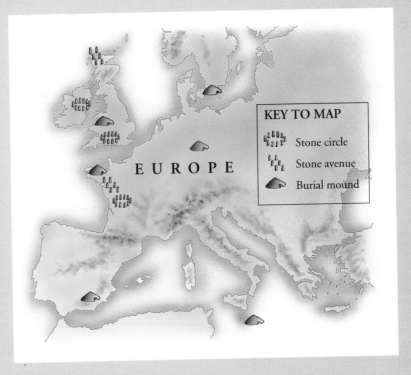

EUROPE

KEY TO MAP

Stone circle

Stone avenue

Burial mound

▼ *Megaliths*
Many monuments consist of megaliths, a word meaning 'big stones'. At Carnac in Brittany, France (below), nearly 1,000 stones were set on end in long rows about 7,000 years ago. They are some of the world's oldest manufactured structures.

Prehistoric tombs at New Grange in Ireland lie hidden under a mound of stones and earth 12 m high, surrounded by a ring of ninety-seven flat stone slabs. For a few days each winter, New Grange reveals its secret. As the sun rises on the shortest day of the year (known as the Winter Solstice), its rays shine straight down the long entrance passage. For a few moments, the domed ceiling of the central chamber glows with strange light and its carved patterns appear to come to life.

Stonehenge, in England, is perhaps the most famous prehistoric monument of all. It was built and rebuilt many times between about 2750 and 1500 BC. The main sandstone blocks at Stonehenge weigh up to 40 tons each. They were quarried about 30 km away, dragged to Stonehenge on wooden rollers, and raised into place using earth ramps and pulleys.

▼ *Stonehenge as it appears today. Nobody can be certain what it looked like in ancient times.*

Stonehenge: the jigsaw puzzle
Each huge upright stone at Stonehenge slots into the horizontal top pieces (lintels) like a plug into a socket. Builders today still use similar methods to hold sections of buildings together.

Stonehenge

Lintel

Mortice

Tenon

Modern timber joint

There are so many stones at Stonehenge that people say if you try and count them, you will never get the same number twice. Some of the smaller stones came from Wales, 240 km away. Stonehenge's builders may have believed that the Welsh blue stone had magical qualities.

The biggest mystery of Stonehenge is why it was built at all. Was it a temple to the sun or moon, or to a snake god? Was it a palace, an assembly hall, or a cemetery? Perhaps it was an observatory for studying the stars, or a huge computer for calculating time and seasons. People once believed that Stonehenge was built by giants or fairies, or by people from a UFO (unidentified flying object) from outer space.

▲ Most ancient monuments are solid, but the Statue of Liberty in New York, USA, is hollow, built round an iron skeleton. It was made in France and shipped to New York in sections in 1885.

Greek Admiration
The Greek poet Hesiod envied the simple life of the prehistoric monument builders. He wrote: 'They lived as if they were gods, their hearts were free from sorrow, and when they died it was just like falling asleep.'

chapter three

ANCIENT MIDDLE EAST

Crashing Walls
There is a famous story in the Bible which describes how the walls of Jericho fell when Joshua blew his trumpet: '. . . and when the army heard the trumpet sound they raised a great shout, and down fell the walls. The army advanced on the city, every man straight ahead, and took it.' (Joshua 6, 20-21)

All over the modern world there are towns and cities where large numbers of people live and work together. Cities provide employment in shops, offices and factories. They usually have good transport and plenty of opportunities for sport and entertainment. But in ancient times, there was another reason for building cities – defence. People felt safer in large numbers, protected by strong walls which they built round their cities.

The first city to be built is believed to be Jericho, in Jordan. The stone walls round Jericho were built almost 10,000 years ago, twice as long ago as the pyramids of Egypt. Almost as old as Jericho was the ancient city of Çatal Hüyük in Turkey.

◄ **Çatal Hüyük**
The houses in Çatal Hüyük were tightly packed together, rising in terraces up the sloping hillsides. In the centre of each group of buildings was an open courtyard, shared by several families.

Archaeologists who have excavated the site of the city have found not only walls, but the remains of mud-brick homes, works of art, fragments of bone, plant pollen, and fabric. There is even a wall painting from about 6200 BC which shows the houses of the city with the nearby volcano Hasan Dag in the background. From their finds, archaeologists can piece together a detailed picture of everyday life in a prehistoric city.

A few thousand years later, a number of much smaller cities rose further to the east of Turkey. These were the powerful city states of Mesopotamia, dating from about 3500 BC, which were the true ancestors of modern towns and cities.

▼ *The modern city of Toronto, Canada, appears to grow out of the waters of Lake Ontario. Although cities today are very different from those built 10,000 years ago, there are many similarities in how they are used.*

Large cities began in Mesopotamia (modern Iraq), because this was the fertile land between the great rivers Tigris and Euphrates. By using the floods to water their rich soil, one family could grow enough food to feed many other people. Since these other people did not need to farm for themselves, they were free to group together and form a city.

The first Mesopotamians built their houses using reeds from the river banks. There are still homes just like this in the swamps of southern Iraq. But in the cities, people soon started to use mud. Mud was strengthened with chopped straw, formed into brick shapes, then left in the hot sun to set hard. Roofs were made from palm logs and leaves. The outer walls of these houses were solid, apart from one doorway. Windows looked inwards on to a shaded central courtyard. Only the larger homes of rich families were two storeys high. These houses had wooden balconies along the upper floors, just like the verandas on houses in hot countries today.

▼ *The Marsh Arabs of southern Iraq today still build their homes from bundles of reeds. This simple but effective method has changed little since ancient times.*

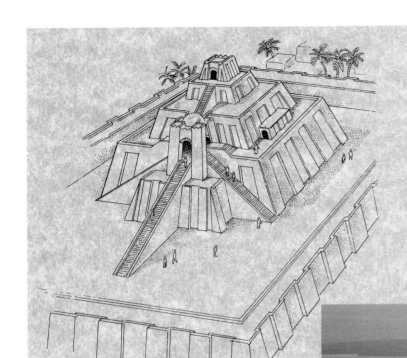

Ancient Skyscrapers

Ziggurats were stepped brick platforms with religious temples perched on the top. The ziggurat at Ur, in modern day Iraq, stood 80 m high and was built in about 2100 BC. It was made mainly of mud bricks, but with fired bricks on the outside for strength. 3,000 years later, the Maya people of Central America built their stone temples in the same shape. The tops of some modern New York skyscrapers have also copied this design.

Almost half of the world's population still lives in mud structures similar to those of the ancient Mesopotamians. They are cheap and easy to build, practical to live in, and they are not harmful to the environment. In some places, like Mali in West Africa, builders today are able to build sophisticated modern structures using ancient mud-building techniques. The Great Mosque at Djenne, Mali, was completed in 1907 and is the world's largest mud building. Where the Mesopotamians used to strengthen their mud walls with chopped straw, the Malians use rice and millet husks to make them more waterproof.

▲ *The Chrysler building in New York looks like a huge ancient ziggurat. When it was built in 1926 it was the world's tallest building. The wheel shapes reminded people of the cars made by the Chrysler Company.*

chapter four

ANCIENT EGYPT

The pyramids of ancient Egypt are among the wonders of the ancient world. Today, 4,500 years after they were built, they still rank alongside the greatest of human achievements. There are few designs in architecture as simple but as strong as the pyramid. With all their sides the same size, pyramids seem to be perfect shapes.

Like most buildings, the pyramids had a purpose – to house the bodies of dead pharaohs (kings). The Egyptians believed that when their body died, their spirit stayed alive as long as the body was kept well and ready to receive it again. Bodies were therefore embalmed, wrapped in cloths and placed in coffins to be mummified.

▼ *The Pyramids of Giza were built in about 2600 BC. The Great Pyramid is 250 m square and stands 150 m high, but the joins between the stones are only 0.5 mm wide.*

◄ *A famous pyramid stands by the entrance to the Louvre museum in Paris. But instead of being solid, it is made of glass, so that each side reflects a different view of the sky. A second glass pyramid has recently been added – but this one perches on its tip, upside down!*

The pharaohs' tombs were hidden in pyramids along with their household goods and treasures. The Egyptians hoped that the strength of the pyramid would protect the tombs from robbers. Spells were written on the walls to help the dead pharaoh's spirit on its way and to curse anyone who disturbed his rest.

Pyramid building – then and now

Few, if any, modern building works can match the skill and organization needed to build the pyramids. According to the Greek writer Herodotus, 100,000 men, fed on onions, worked for twenty years to build the great Pyramid of Cheops. Even the largest construction company today would take just as long to do the same work using modern methods and machinery.

▲ *The tops of columns on buildings today are often decorated with carved leaves. This practice goes back to the Egyptians, who believed that their land had grown like a plant from the sea. The Egyptians decorated their own columns to look like plants, such as the papyrus and lotus flowers.*

Nobody knows for certain why pyramids were built where they were. Tomb paintings suggest that they may have been positioned to represent a huge map of the stars which were most important to the pharaohs.

Two narrow shafts lead out of the king's and queen's tombs in the Great Pyramid at Giza. It used to be thought that these were air vents. But scientists have now calculated that when the pyramid was built, in about 2600 BC, these shafts must have pointed directly at Orion (the king's star) and Sirius (the queen's star). Perhaps the Egyptians wanted to use the rays of the stars' light to carry the spirits of the dead king and queen up to the heavens.

Modern religious beliefs often influence the architecture of buildings just as Egyptian beliefs did. The peaceful interior of Buddhist temples helps people to meditate by focusing on the image of the Buddha. Muslim mosques point towards the holy city of Mecca. Christian churches are often cross-shaped to remind people that Jesus Christ died for their sins. Most churches also point east. This is a legacy of the ancient practice of making temples point towards the rising sun.

Ancient Greek visitors were amazed by the pyramids, but it was the Egyptian temples which most influenced their own buildings. The massive columns we can still see at Karnak today were carved in sections. The sections were piled on top of each other to form columns. Huge stone slabs were placed across the top to bridge the gaps, like the lintel stones at Stonehenge a thousand years earlier. These techniques, first developed by the ancient Egyptians, were perfected by the Greeks, then the Romans, and are still in use today.

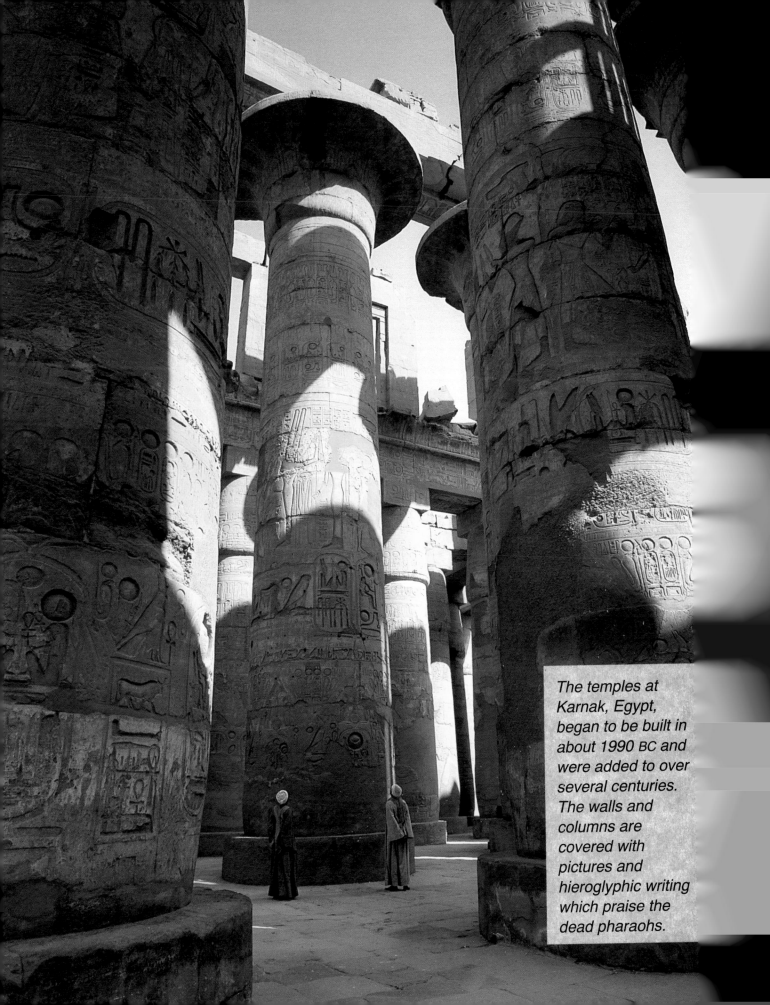

The temples at Karnak, Egypt, began to be built in about 1990 BC and were added to over several centuries. The walls and columns are covered with pictures and hieroglyphic writing which praise the dead pharaohs.

chapter five

ANCIENT GREECE

Many modern towns and cities in the Western world have buildings which look like ancient Greek temples. Instead of being temples to gods like Zeus or Athene, they might be important government buildings, like the White House in Washington, USA, or famous churches, like St Peter's in Rome, Italy. They might be theatres, like the Bolshoi in Moscow, Russia, or museums, like the British Museum in London, England.

The style adapted from Greek temples is often called 'classical' architecture. It was first copied by the Romans. Since then, people all over the world have copied this style of building, right down to our own times. They have used it for important public buildings,

▼ *The Acropolis in Athens, Greece, stands on a natural hill which was raised to form a level platform. This ensured that the temples and statues could be seen from all over the city of Athens, and can still be seen today.*

but also for ordinary houses. When the Greeks developed their classical style, they were influenced by the Egyptians.

Greek traders were impressed by the temples and tombs they saw in Egypt. Back home, they gradually developed their own style of temple building, using the fine white marble of their country. The Greek buildings were in some ways quite unlike those in Egypt. This is because ancient Greece and Egypt were very different countries. In Egypt, one great king could command 100,000 men to build a single tomb. But Greece was made up of small islands and city states, each with its own ruler. Their temples were therefore built on a smaller scale.

▲ *The City Hall in Birmingham, England, was designed in 1832 to look like an ancient Greek temple.*

▲ *If you look closely at the pillars of the Parthenon in Athens, Greece, you can see how precisely each stone was carved.*

The structure of Greek temples was not new. It used lines of columns to prop up the roof, with single stone blocks in between. This was no different from Egyptian, or even prehistoric buildings. What the Greeks perfected was a sense of proportion and symmetry which has never been improved on to this day. They used precise mathematical rules to fix the dimensions of buildings. Having decided, for example, how wide to build a temple, the rules told them how long and high it should be, how thick to make the columns, and what gaps to leave between them.

Greek temples were built so solidly that many have survived to the present day. You can visit them not only in Greece, but also in the parts of Asia and southern Italy which were once ruled by the Greeks. The temple at Syracuse, in Sicily, was built 2,400 years ago and is still in use as a Christian church.

The strong, simple form of the Parthenon in Athens, Greece, looks best when seen against the sky from below. Its rectangular shape is misleading. All the columns are in fact tapered and tip inwards so that the whole building is

◄ *The Parthenon in Athens, Greece, perhaps the most famous temple of all. Designed in 447 BC, it still stands on the Acropolis, a high hill overlooking the city of Athens.*

slightly pyramid-shaped. There are no exact right angles anywhere in the Parthenon. Nor are any two blocks of marble exactly the same, though each has a mirror image on the opposite side. Each column was made in ten or twelve pieces, then ground together to make a perfect fit and joined with plugs and sockets. So Greek temples like the Parthenon are not really the simple shapes they appear to be.

Palladio

The Italian architect Andrea Palladio (1508–80) adapted Greek rules of proportion to suit smaller buildings. Thanks to Palladio, many ordinary homes built in Europe and America owe their appearance to the ancient Greeks.

In 1769, the American President Thomas Jefferson used Palladio's ideas to design his own house at Monticello, USA. ►

The classical style as we know it today is easy to recognize, whether or not the buildings look like temples. The style looks equally good whether it is used for a great palace, like Versailles in France, or a humble terraced house. What these have in common are perfect proportions and symmetry. The door stands exactly in the centre of the front wall. An equal number of windows is placed symmetrically on either side. Windows are usually of the sash type, which slide up and down instead of having hinges. These suit the classical proportions better.

Sometimes there is a pediment (triangular shape) like the pediment at each end of a temple over the door or under the roof. Pediments are often held up by columns, or mock columns called pilasters. Again, these are meant to add to the balanced effect and remind us of temple columns.

▼ *This is Chiswick House in London, England. It was built in 1725, and used the architect Palladio's Villa Rotunda in Italy as a model. The Villa Rotunda was built nearly 200 years earlier, in 1550.*

Very big classical-style houses often have porticos in the centre. Porticos are big pillared porches round the front door, but look almost like miniature temples in themselves. They became popular in eighteenth-century houses like Chiswick House in London, England (above), built in 1725. Their owners thought that rich people in ancient times had built porticos to show how important they were.

Greek Classical Columns

Doric   Ionic   Corinthian

◄ The Greeks developed three distinct styles of column – the Doric, the Ionic and the Corinthian. The Doric was the earliest design and had a shaft which tapered directly from the floor, appearing to grow straight out of the ground. The Doric's capital (top) was plain. The Ionic and Corinthian styles are more elegant, slender in relation to their height and crowned with graceful capitals which look like scrolls of leaves.

Inside modern homes there are machines, technology, conveniences and comforts which the Greeks could not even dream of 2,500 years ago. But on the outside, modern houses with classical architecture have a balanced design, with the shapes of windows, doors and other features still based on those of ancient Greek temples.

◄ Modern domestic houses such as this one are quite small. However, classical features like pillars and pediments give them an appearance of grandeur.

chapter six

ANCIENT ROME

In ancient times, visitors to the Greek lands of the eastern Mediterranean were impressed by the beauty of Greek temples and public buildings. The Romans, in particular, developed the classical style in striking new ways. As their powerful empire expanded from North Africa to the borders of Scotland, the Romans spread their skills in design, technology and organization.

The legacy of the Romans is all over Europe and beyond. There is Hadrian's Wall, a massive defensive barrier built right across northern England in AD 122. Roman public

▼ *The Pont du Gard was built in AD 14. It once carried water to the Roman city of Nimes in Southern France. Its huge stone arches were a triumph of Roman engineering skill.*

buildings are still in use, like the Porta Nigra in Trier, Germany, or the Pont du Gard bridge in France. Italy, and the city of Rome itself, probably contain the greatest number of Roman buildings.

Many roads across Europe today use the same routes which Roman surveyors and road builders first mapped out 2,000 years ago. Many European towns and cities were founded in Roman times and have been lived in ever since.

▲ At Pompeii in southern Italy, you can still walk down a Roman street and step into Roman houses like the one above. They have been preserved by lava and ash which covered the city when the nearby volcano Vesuvius erupted in AD 79. This 'cubiculum' (bedroom) obviously belonged to a wealthy Roman, with its highly decorated walls and mosaic floor.

Soldiers and builders
Seneca, a famous Roman writer, described the genius of his people. He said: 'The Romans came into the world with a sword in one hand and a spade in the other.'

▼ *Roman soldiers built Hadrian's Wall, England, in AD 122. Forts and look-out posts were placed at regular intervals to help defend against attacks from the north.*

Roman architecture was more practical than Greek architecture. For a long time the Romans used Greek ideas of beauty to decorate their buildings. But the Romans were more interested in power, so they wanted to build the strongest structures for their buildings. Some of the Romans' finest work was in buiulding aqueducts, bridges or similar practical structures.

Rome and its empire had a much greater population than Greece. Most Romans preferred to live in towns and cities rather than the countryside. The splendid architecture of their great cities reminded the people they conquered, such as the Celts of northern Europe, that it would be dangerous to offend their Roman rulers.

Centuries later, when the British founded an even larger empire, they used architecture in a similar way, to impose their authority on the people they ruled. In this way, the buildings the British erected in India, part of their empire, owe more to Roman styles than to traditional Indian ideas.

▲ *Fort St George looks like a typical public building from ancient Rome. In fact, it was built by the British in the Indian city of Madras, when India was part of the British Empire, 1,500 years after the end of the Roman Empire.*

Roman buildings sometimes looked less refined and delicate than those of the Greeks, but they were very strong. Many Roman public buildings were far too big for the old post and lintel methods. Slender Greek-style columns were, and still are, popular as decoration, but they were not strong enough to support the great weight of larger Roman constructions. Nor could they be used to span the much greater widths needed for huge halls and bridges. Instead the Romans turned to the arch.

A truthful builder
The Roman bridge at Alcantra, Spain, has the inscription 'Pontem perfeci mansurum in saecula' (I have built a bridge to last for centuries). This is certainly true – it was built in AD 105 and is still in use.

31

The arch is a very simple device. It allows builders to use quite small stone blocks or even bricks to cross gaps that would be too long to span by other means.

This simple technique enabled the Romans to build great bridges and aqueducts, many of which are still standing. Similar methods are in use to this day, but they have now been adapted for building with materials such as iron, steel and concrete.

▲ Building an arch
Builders in Moscow, Russia, recently built an arch using the same techniques as the Romans developed, nearly 2,000 years ago. First, a light-weight wooden frame is built in the shape of the arch. This is used as a temporary support while the bricks or stones are fixed in place. Once the final 'keystone' is in place at the top, the support can be taken away and the arch supports itself.

The Romans' next step was to develop simple arches into vaults and domes. These enabled Roman builders to hold up roofs over great spaces without the need for hundreds of props littering the floor. The simplest vault was like a tunnel of arches built in a line. The passages inside Roman amphitheatres, like the Colosseum in Rome, were usually made like this. It is very strong, although the walls need to be extremely thick to prevent them being pushed outwards by the weight of the vaults above.

To solve this problem, the Romans developed cross vaults. These helped to direct the forces straight down the walls rather than outwards. In turn, this meant that walls could become thinner and contain large open arches or windows. This was the method used by the builders of the Baths of Diocletian in Rome. The method was so strong that you can still see the Baths as they stand today, now used as a church.

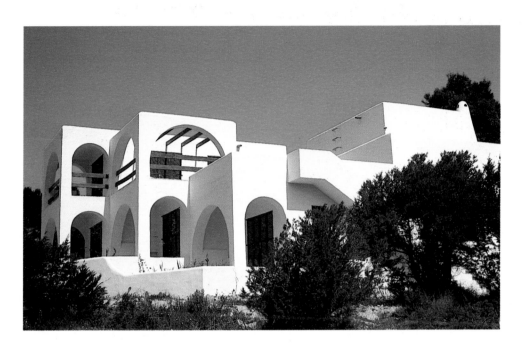

◄ *These modern holiday villas in Ibiza, Spain, show Romanesque arches of Moorish architecture. The Moors, who ruled North Africa and Spain after the Romans, inherited the Roman style of arch and we can still see its influence today.*

Long after the end of the Roman Empire, builders continued to use these methods to erect the great churches and cathedrals of medieval and modern times. Those with round (rather than pointed) arches are still called Romanesque, which reminds us of our debt to the Roman inventors of these methods.

▼ *The Colosseum in Rome was built in AD 70–80. It seated up to 50,000 people watching gladiators and wild animals fight to the death. The outer walls were 50 m high, with three rows of vaulted corridors running round the edge and inwards. These gave easy access to all areas of seating.*

▲ *The huge 'eye' at the top of the Pantheon's dome reminded the Romans of the sun at the centre of the universe.*

Roman concrete
In the third century BC, Roman builders first discovered how to make concrete by mixing together volcanic ash, lime, sand, gravel and water. The mixture dried to become a sort of artificial rock. This was waterproof and solid, and could be set into any shape. The Romans poured it into brick compartments. Their method was the strongest until steel rods were developed in the nineteenth century.

Domes were another idea developed by the Romans from the arch and vault. Domes are really just circles of arches which all meet in the middle. The largest dome built by the Romans is the Pantheon in Rome, built in about AD 120 as a temple for all the gods. At the very top there is a circular hole which lets light into the vast space below. From the ground the hole looks small, but it is big enough for a bus to go through. To reduce weight, the walls are hollow and get thinner higher up. The dome has a thin outer layer built on a skeleton of strong ribs. This great engineering achievement has been copied right down to the present day – a good example is the huge domed cathedral built by 'Emperor' Bokhassa in central Africa in the 1980s.

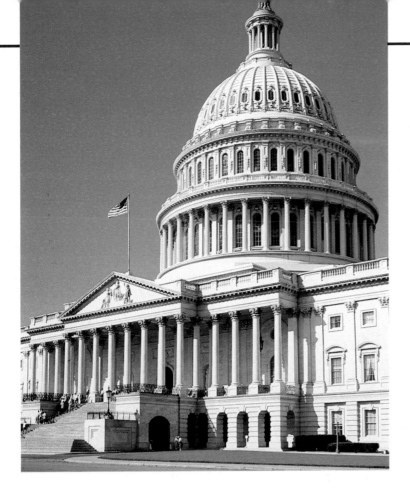

The Colosseum and Pantheon, like many Roman buildings, would never have been possible without another great invention – concrete. Concrete was used to fill the 12 m deep foundations of the Colosseum. Most of its walls and vaults were also solid concrete, with bricks on the surface. The rings of the Pantheon's dome are also made of concrete.

Concrete is not a pretty material so the Romans improved its appearance by covering its surface with bricks, marble or mosaic patterns. Modern concrete buildings are often covered in the same way. Sydney Opera House, built in 1959–73, is made of arched concrete shells covered with white ceramic tiles. Today, concrete is still used much as the Romans used it, but it is strengthened with steel rods.

▲ *The Capitol building in Washington DC, USA, shows how a dome makes a building stand out and look important. This dome was added in 1851, sixty years after the main building was begun.*

▶ *Sydney Opera House in Australia is one of the world's most famous modern buildings. But its strength and shape depend on the ancient Roman inventions of concrete and arched vaulting.*

▶ *St Clement's temple in Rome is an early Christian church. Its design copied a Roman meeting place or basilica (below). You can see the apse at the end and the columns down the sides which separate the side compartments.*

▼ *Plan of a typical Roman basilica.*

Just as most of today's religions, like Judaism, Hinduism, Buddhism and Christianity, began in ancient times, so did the design of religious buildings. However, for the Christian religion, Roman temples were not a suitable model because inside, there was only a small room or shrine containing the god's statue. Christian worship needed more space because it practised inside a building. So instead of temples, Roman assembly halls, called basilicas, provided a better model for Christian churches. The traditional basilica was an oblong shape. It had narrow compartments down the sides, separated from the main hall by columns, like a covered street of shops. At the far end was a raised semi-circular section called an apse, where the officials sat.

The Roman basilica was an ideal shape for Christian worship. The church altar was placed in the apse, which was reserved for the officials, or priests. The people gathered in the main body of the basilica, now called the nave, just as the Romans had done for other sorts of meetings.

The legacy of ancient Rome has affected smaller homes as well as big public buildings. The beautiful houses of wealthy Romans, with their mosaic floors, open courtyards, scented formal gardens and efficient plumbing and heating systems, have provided a model for gracious living ever since. Less wealthy Romans, however, lived in cheaply built blocks of flats up to six storeys high. In modern cities, a lack of space has required similar apartment blocks to be built, designed to house many people in a small space.

▲ *This fresco, from a villa in Pompeii, shows a Roman street, crowded with houses.*

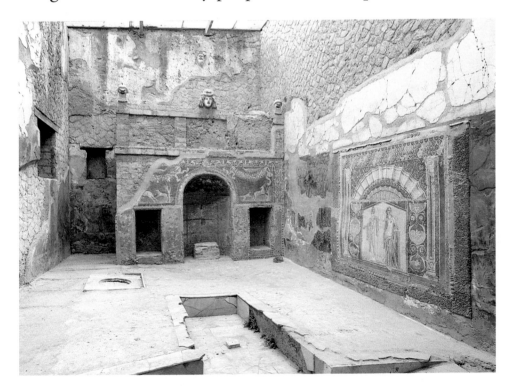

◄ *The houses of wealthy Romans usually had a central courtyard. This one, in a house in Herculaneum, Italy, is also an open-air dining room. A mosaic plaque decorates one wall. The mosaic represents the sea-god Neptune and Amphitrite, his wife.*

chapter seven

ANCIENT
CELTS

The cool, moist climate of northern Europe provides ideal conditions for trees to grow. Since ancient times, the temperate zones of Europe, North America, China, Japan and Southeast Asia, have been the home of timber-building traditions.

Modern timber-framed houses often use treated softwoods like fir or spruce, but hard woods like oak make an even stronger building material. Oak is easy to cut when green, but dries out to an iron-like toughness. This was the wood preferred by the Celts of northern Europe, 3,000 years ago.

▲ *This cottage in Normandy, France, uses timber framing and reed thatch in much the same way as the Celts did 2,000 years ago.*

The Roman writer Strabo described the houses of the Celts: 'Their houses are large and circular, built of planks and wickerwork, the roof being a dome of heavy thatch.'

The building methods of the Celts were used over the centuries, almost until our own times. Perhaps the only reason why they are no longer widely practised is that since about AD 1700, trees have been in short supply and bricks have become cheaper.

We know enough about Celtic timber buildings from archaeological remains to be able to reconstruct them very accurately. One reason why the originals no longer survive is that they were constructed around wooden posts set directly into the ground. Over time, these posts have rotted away, leaving only marks in the soil where they once stood.

Later timber houses, from about AD 1300 onwards, were usually built on low brick or stone walls. These gave better protection from the damp earth, and many such buildings still exist for us to see. The steep straw or reed-thatched roofs of these later houses also came from Celtic methods and thatched roofs are still in use today in many parts of the world.

▲ *The Akha tribe in Thailand like the Celts 2,000 years ago have made use of the most easily available material to build their houses – trees from the natural forest of northern Thailand.*

▼ *These buildings at Butser, England, are modern models of ancient Celtic round houses.*

Wattle and daub
The Celts filled the gaps between their upright timbers with woven panels of sticks (wattles). On to these they splattered a mixture of mud, clay, straw and cow dung (daub) which set hard when dry.

chapter eight

ANCIENT ASIA

Just as Christian church architecture is still based on ancient models, in Asia too, the design of modern temples, such as the Lakshmi Nerain in New Delhi, is based on the ancient traditions of the Hindu and Buddhist faiths.

By 1500 BC, many people in India were already living in cities. These were often far larger than those in Mesopotamia, with carefully planned streets of two-storey houses, built of kiln-fired bricks. Their early temples

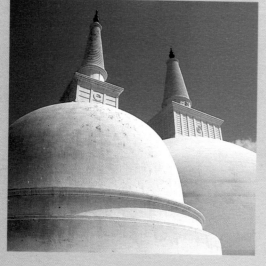

▲ *These Buddhist stupas in Anuradhapura, the ancient capital of Sri Lanka, are over 2,000 years old. They are built of sun-dried mud bricks and painted white to reflect the sun.*

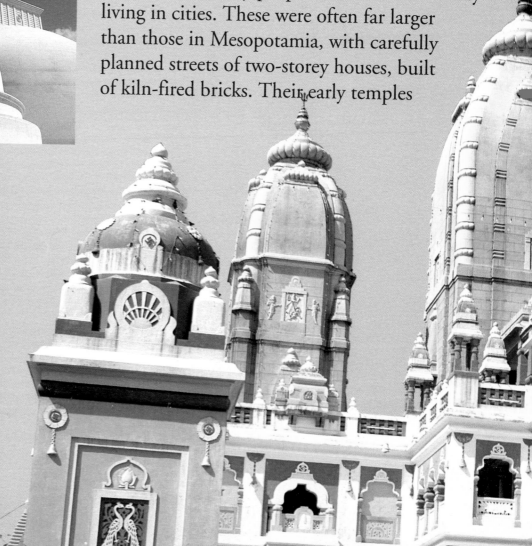

were made of wood rather than brick. However, with the spread of Buddhism from the fifth century BC onwards, temples were often built of brick or stone. Their design exactly copied that of the earlier wooden structures, right down to imitating the shape of their wooden beams.

The Buddhist stupa was originally a simple dome, built to house the remains of the Buddha and his followers. Soon stupas were extended upwards. Their tall towers had many storeys, each with a separate, umbrella-shaped roof. These towers were meant to represent the axis (line) on which the world turned. The stupa at Peshawur was over 200 m high, and topped with twenty-five rows of copper umbrellas.

Buddhism was the religion of merchants who traded far across the mountains of Tibet into China. Wherever they went, they took their religion and its distinctive architecture. In China and Japan, the Buddhist stupa soon developed into the distinctive oriental style of the pagoda. Pagodas, with their great curved roofs overhanging the walls, in turn influenced the design of other buildings.

▲ Pagoda-shaped buildings are all over the world today. Many cities like Sydney, Australia (above) and New York, USA have a Chinatown area where communities of Chinese and Japanese people live. They decorate their buildings in the traditional oriental styles which date back to ancient times.

▼ The skyline of this modern temple in Delhi, India, is based on architectural ideas going back almost 2,500 years.

▼ *Perhaps the most remarkable of all ancient Chinese buildings was not a temple but a wall. The Great Wall of China was completed by the Emperor Tsin Shi Hwang Di in 214 BC. He was the first ruler of all China, and built the wall to protect his country against nomadic tribes from the north. The wall stretches for 2,250 km across northern China. It is 7 m high and has 25,000 watch towers, each 14 m tall, at regular intervals. It is the only artifical structure which can be seen from outer space.*

In the great cities of Asia today, builders usually prefer the Western style of skyscrapers and apartment blocks. But you can still find many reminders of ancient styles in older buildings, and local architects often try to combine traditional and modern methods.

It was not until the fifteenth century that Europeans first set eyes on the wonders of the Far East. They were amazed by the beauty of oriental silk clothing and shiny glazed pottery (still called 'china'), as well as the elegant Asian houses and temples with distinctively curved roofs. Ideas and illustrations began to filter through, along with goods like silks, spices and a herbal drink called tea.

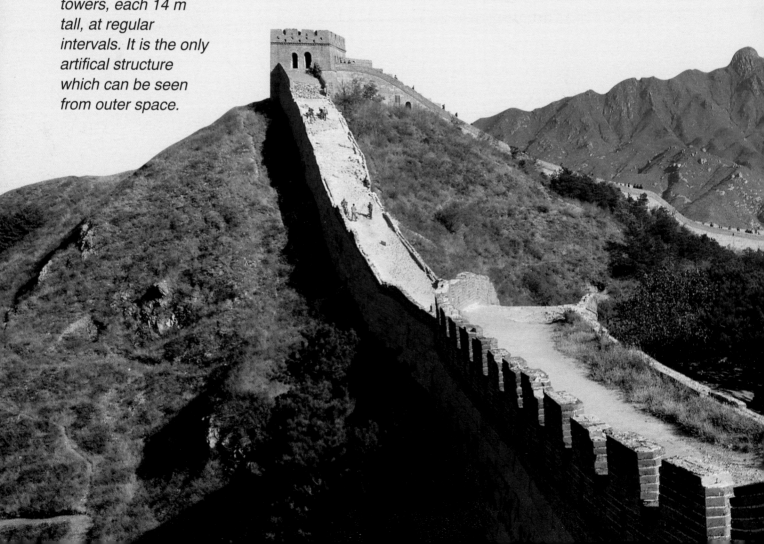

By the 1700s, oriental goods and styles were fashionable amongst wealthy people across Europe. No country mansion was complete without its 'chinoiserie' room, with oriental-style wallpaper, furniture and decorations. Sometimes the fashion even spread to the buildings themselves, such as at the Royal Pavilion in Brighton, England. Here, in the early 1800s, the Prince Regent extended his seaside house with an amazing mixture of styles from India, China and Japan. Queen Victoria later did the same in the Indian rooms at Osborne House.

▲ *Even the chimneys of Brighton's Royal Pavilion, in England, are designed to look like the towers of an Indian temple.*

Northern Europe

Before 3000 BC	2000 BC	1000 BC	0	AD

15000
●
Cave paintings
of simple huts,
France

3000
●
First stone circles,
Western Europe

800
●
Iron first
used in
Europe

122
●
Hadrian's Wall,
Britain

6000
●
First farmers
in Europe

500
●
Celtic lake
villages in
Austria

4500
●
First stone
monuments,
Brittany

2750
●
Stonehenge
construction
started,
Britain

1500
●
Stonehenge
construction
finished,
Britain

4000
●
Flint mined
in Britain

Far East and Americas

Before 3000 BC	2000 BC	1000 BC	0	AD

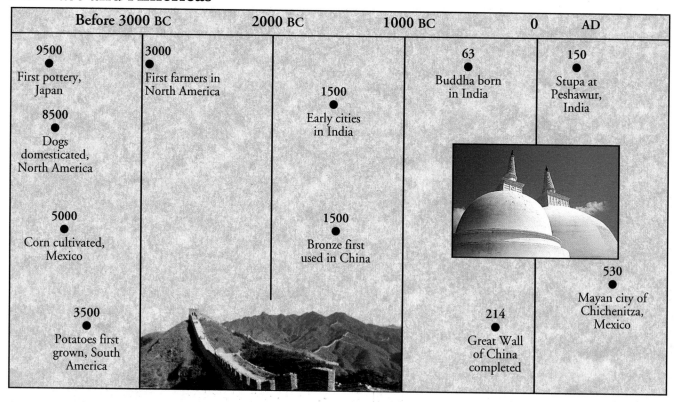

9500
●
First pottery,
Japan

3000
●
First farmers in
North America

63
●
Buddha born
in India

150
●
Stupa at
Peshawur,
India

8500
●
Dogs
domesticated,
North America

1500
●
Early cities
in India

5000
●
Corn cultivated,
Mexico

1500
●
Bronze first
used in China

530
●
Mayan city of
Chichenitza,
Mexico

3500
●
Potatoes first
grown, South
America

214
●
Great Wall
of China
completed

The Middle East

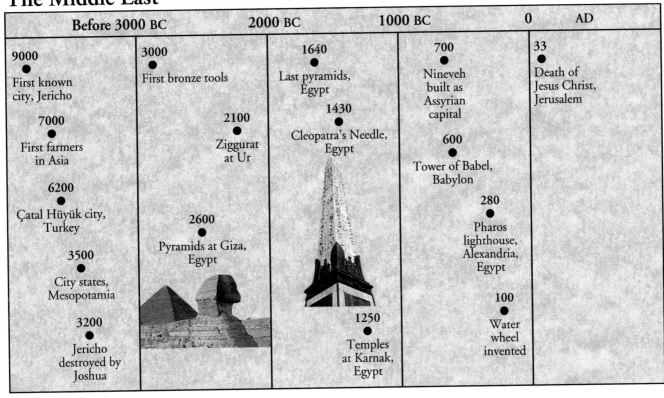

Before 3000 BC	2000 BC	1000 BC	0	AD
9000 First known city, Jericho	**3000** First bronze tools	**1640** Last pyramids, Egypt	**700** Nineveh built as Assyrian capital	**33** Death of Jesus Christ, Jerusalem
7000 First farmers in Asia	**2100** Ziggurat at Ur	**1430** Cleopatra's Needle, Egypt	**600** Tower of Babel, Babylon	
6200 Çatal Hüyük city, Turkey	**2600** Pyramids at Giza, Egypt		**280** Pharos lighthouse, Alexandria, Egypt	
3500 City states, Mesopotamia		**1250** Temples at Karnak, Egypt	**100** Water wheel invented	
3200 Jericho destroyed by Joshua				

The Mediterranean Lands

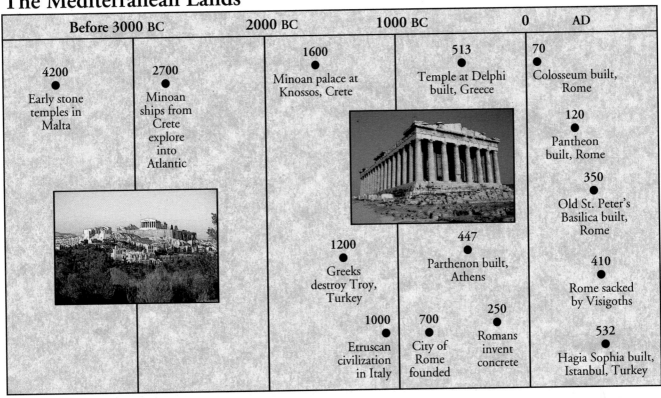

Before 3000 BC	2000 BC	1000 BC	0	AD
4200 Early stone temples in Malta	**1600** Minoan palace at Knossos, Crete	**513** Temple at Delphi built, Greece	**70** Colosseum built, Rome	
2700 Minoan ships from Crete explore into Atlantic			**120** Pantheon built, Rome	
	1200 Greeks destroy Troy, Turkey	**447** Parthenon built, Athens	**350** Old St. Peter's Basilica built, Rome	
	1000 Etruscan civilization in Italy	**700** City of Rome founded	**410** Rome sacked by Visigoths	
		250 Romans invent concrete	**532** Hagia Sophia built, Istanbul, Turkey	

GLOSSARY

Aqueducts   Bridges for carrying water above ground.

Amphitheatres   Circular or oval meeting places for performances.

Apse   A rounded end to a rectangular building.

Archaeologists   People who study ancient remains.

Balconies   Raised platforms attached to the wall of a building.

Basilicas   Oblong-shaped meeting halls.

Buddha   The founder of Buddhism who lived in about 563–483 BC.

Chinoiserie   Chinese style.

Domestic   To do with homes and families.

Embalmed   Preserved from decay with special fluids.

Fertile   Fruitful, or good for growing crops.

Fragments   Small pieces, often broken off from a larger object.

Megaliths   Large stones used as monuments.

Mummified   When a body is dried to preserve its shape.

Nave   The main body of a church building.

Observatory   A place for studying the sky and stars.

Oriental   From Asia.

Pagodas   Tall towers with many roofs at different levels.

Pediments   Triangular roof shapes over doors, windows or pillars.

Pilasters   Decoration which looks like pillars.

Pollen   A dusty substance which plants use for fertilization.

Prehistoric   From the earliest times before written records.

Proportion   How sizes and shapes relate to each other.

Romanesque   Roman-style architecture.

Solstice   When the sun rises for the longest or shortest times of the year.

Sophisticated   Carefully planned, or complicated.

Stupa   A dome-shaped temple building.

Symmetry   Equality on both sides of a dividing line.

Tapered   Narrowing towards one end.

Temperate zones   Regions which are never very hot or very cold, where trees grow well.

Vaults   Arch-shaped ceilings.

Vents   Openings for ventilation.

Ziggurats   Stepped towers.

BOOKS TO READ

There are many books about individual ancient civilizations. These books explain more general developments in ancient architecture.

The Atlas of Ancient Worlds by A. Millard (Dorling Kindersley, 1994)

The Atlas of the Ancient World by M. Oliphant (Ebury Press, 1992)

The Kingfisher Book of How they were Built by D. Brown (Kingfisher, 1991)

The Visual Dictionary of Buildings by Courtenay-Thompson (Ed.) (Dorling Kindersley, 1992)

A Town Through History by X. Hernandez & P. Comes (Wayland, 1993)

The Earliest Civilizations by M. Oliphant (Simon & Schuster, 1993)

The Builder Through History by R. Wood (Wayland, 1994)

Picture acknowledgements:
The publishers would like to thank the following for allowing their pictures to be used in this book:
Ancient Art & Architecture Collection 9, 28-29; Eye Ubiquitous 5 (top right), 20, 25 (top), 36, 38, 40, 44 (bottom right), 45 (bottom right); Robert Harding 5 (top left), 6, 8, 9, 16, 25 (bottom), 31, 33 (top), 39 (top), 45 (top right); Images Colour Library 42-43, 44; Tony Stone Worldwide *Cover (main),* 4 (top, second & third down), 7, 10 (top), 10-11, 12-13, 13 (top), 14-15, 18-19, 21, 22-23, 23 (top), 26, 27, 30, 33, 34, 35 (top & bottom), 40-41, 43 (top); Werner Forman Archive 4 (top), 24, 29, 37 (top & bottom), 38-39, 44 (top right); Richard Wood 32; Wayland Picture Library 4 (bottom), 5 (bottom), 45 (top left & bottom left); Zefa *Cover (inset),* 17, 19 (top), 44 (top left).
All artwork is by Peter Bull.

INDEX

Numbers in **bold** refer to illustrations.